To Denise –
Many blessings
To a dear friend
And confidant.
Sue Storm

Angel First Aid

for
Miracles

SUE STORM

The Angel Lady

Designed by DebManning Design

Manufactured in the United States of America

Revised Edition

ISBN 0-9675291-0-7

The Angel Lady™ is a registered trademark of
Angelight Productions

Message from Archangel Michael

Angel First Aid was created to provide guidance and understanding to all who are seeking a more meaningful life. We, the Angels, take great joy in contributing to your pursuit of happiness. With Angelic blessings, miracles will begin to happen.

ACKNOWLEDGMENTS

Writing this book has been a labor of love for so many people. It could not have been accomplished without the dedicated efforts of Conni Pluchino, Deborah Hawkins, Laura Black, Richard Dilworth and Milad Nourahmadi, my "Angel Assistants."

The guidance and suggestions received from Annie Hall, Michelle Farina, Cyd Franks, Sharon Kissane and Marsha Portnoy have been extremely beneficial. Mary Doyle Brodien, Marcia DeFalco, Denise Gierach, Linda Howe, Ruth Kalas and Charles Shaw are also being thanked for their help as catalysts in getting this project started.

Appreciation is extended to my friends and clients whose generous encouragement has been particularly heart warming – especially Vickie Farina, Thelma Fastner, Maggie Fox, David Moravec, Paul Stillman, Sandy Forty, Kyle Koch, Ann Jagert and Chuck LaFrano.

My gratitude is also extended to Carol Canova, Anne Simon-Wolf, Maxine Jones, Genevieve Paulson and Alice Umbach who have served as my teachers and mentors throughout the years. They all played a major role in helping me to achieve my life's purpose.

Thank you to my family: Major and Anita Belkin, Bernie and Tiki, Steve and Joan, Julie, Amy, Hadar, Rinat and Michael. Andy Belkin and Hannah Storm are being acknowledged for their support. Much love goes to my daughter, Rochelle, who has inspired me to write.

Mayor George Pradel (Naperville, Illinois) is being acknowledged because we share a great admiration for the Angels.

To those in the media who have contributed to my career: Nancy Skinner, Stewart Bailey, Dan Lloyd, Paul Myers, Ann Masters, Nancy Wallace, David Ruben, Jack Olson, Chana Bernstein and Oprah Winfrey who lives my dream of being able to help people.

My appreciation to those at Borders Books and their Community Relations Coordinators Mark Moder, Mary Miles, Keloryn Putnam, Kristine Sohacki and Don Weigand who have been instrumental in the success of my Angel presentations. Heartfelt gratitude is also extended to Kelley Wardzala for her many valuable suggestions.

A special thank you to God, "My Little Man" and the Angels, for in truth, *Angel First Aid, Rx for Miracles* is their work.

Dedication

*To all the people who have contributed to the success of the
Angel First Aid Techniques and the popularity of this book.
My gratitude also goes to those who have shared their
miracle stories and Angelic experiences.*

TABLE OF CONTENTS

The Angel Lady

Everyone is born with unique gifts. My special talents are the ability to see, sense and communicate with the Angels. During the past fifteen years, through lectures, seminars, Angel Parties and counseling sessions, I have had the privilege of showing thousands of individuals how to transform their lives through Angelic connections.

My story begins in East Grand Rapids, Michigan at approximately eighteen months of age. In my crib, wrapped up in blankets to the point of almost suffocating, I had a near-death experience. Bright, white objects appeared near the ceiling and a sense of peace came over me. At the same time, I knew that I was going to be saved. It turned out that what I had seen flying above me were Angels.

When I was four years old, a strong sense of special guidance in the form of a voice I called "My Little Man" came into my life. He told me about events that would take place in the future and how to make things happen. Growing up, I trusted his advice. At ten years old, "My Little Man" revealed to me that, as an adult, I would speak to large audiences and not be nervous. Amazingly, this has all come to pass. "My Little Man" still talks to me often and is a constant friend and companion.

After attending the University of Michigan, I got married, raised a daughter and later moved to Naperville, Illinois. In the Spring of 1985, an extraordinary event occurred that changed the course of my life. One day while checking inventory in the warehouse of the company I owned, the ceiling separated and a booming voice called out, *"Sue, you have to help people!"* Every cell in my body resonated with the power that came from this sound. Awestruck, yet feeling calm, I looked up and saw a cloud of fine mist coming through the opening. My immediate response was, *"Yes, God ... what do you want me to do?"*

Although the answer did not come right away, the next few years were very exciting, as my purpose became clear. Giving lectures and providing counseling in the area of prosperity was certainly a way I could carry out God's Divine instructions to "help people." Based on my definition of prosperity, which is the achievement of success in every facet of one's life, I assisted many in improving their lifestyles.

In the Fall of 1996, "My Little Man" told me to "make a writing room." Listening to his advice, I began working on the project. The Divine Plan was for both Barbara Mark and Trudy Griswold (authors of *Angelspeake,* a best-selling guide on communicating with Angels) to use this writing room for their second book. As we spent time together, these special women provided me with many answers – most importantly, "My Little Man" was, in fact, Archangel Michael! He had been guiding me all along towards making the Angels and prosperity my life's work.

Angels are great at public relations, presenting me with countless media opportunities. I have been featured in many newspapers as well as interviewed on numerous radio and television programs. While filming a segment of *The Daily Show,* for *Comedy Central,* the staff began to call me, "**The Angel Lady**." Now, both national and local audiences refer to me by this name. It is also in the title of my cable TV series, *A Visit with The Angel Lady.*

The Angels have kept me very busy giving interviews, seminars, lectures and workshops. While answering thousands of questions, I realized that people needed to have a simple way to collaborate with the Angels and make their lives more enjoyable. Out of this awareness, *Angel First Aid* was born. The wisdom that has come to me through Angelic guidance, I offer to you with all my love.

How to Use This Book

Angel First Aid is a guide to seeking the counsel of Angels and benefiting from their loving involvement. In this book you will learn how to enhance your life by communicating with Celestial Beings. Practicing the exercises, which are referred to as "remedies," furthers your progress. Performing the techniques improves your physical, mental, emotional, financial and spiritual well-being. Using Angel First Aid as a daily reference or handbook has a cumulative effect. By making a connection with the Angelic Realm, you will feel continually supported and blessed.

Simple to Use

This book is separated into six parts, each providing guidance that will help increase your understanding and ability to bond with the Angels. By gaining clarity from performing the remedies, you can begin implementing positive changes and bring joy into your life.

**Frequently Asked Questions about Angels** addresses the subjects that have been brought up during my many lectures and seminars. This section gives an explanation of Celestial Beings, reveals why they were created and describes how they can be of assistance in improving your life.

**Miracle Stories** are accounts of actual encounters with Angels. Sometimes these divine episodes occur as simple coincidences, other times Angelic interventions are more dramatic. Yet all such experiences are truly miracles because of their power to heal and transform.

The main section of the book consists of ten chapters covering _**Prosperity, Relationships, Money, Health, Happiness, Inner Peace, Career, Business, Parenting**_ and _**Pets**_. These topics have been selected because they reflect the areas in which the majority of people have expressed the most interest.

The _**Glossary of Angels**_ is a "Who's Who" for the Angelic Realm. It is a useful alphabetical listing, complete with a description of each Angel's area of expertise. Many of the Celestial Beings not listed in the chapters appear in the glossary.

**Remedies by Chapter** is a guide to the techniques, exercises and visualizations in this book. All the remedies are listed by chapter and in the order necessary to achieve the desired results.

The _**Index**_ includes remedies that can be looked up according to

a referenced keyword. It serves as an integral part of the book. Using the index will increase the benefits of the _Angel First Aid_ Techniques.

Angel First Aid Remedies

A chapters features remedies for making positive changes in your life. A remedy can be an action, visualization or other technique. Recommended dosages are provided for optimal results.

In addition to suggested remedies, each chapter includes:

• Introduction – overview of the subject and explanation of how *Angel First Aid* Techniques can be helpful.

• Angel Specialists – list of Celestial Beings with descriptions of their areas of expertise.

• Affirmations – statements that produce positive effects on the mind, body and spirit.

• Case Studies – real life stories where *Angel First Aid* remedies have been successful.

• Preventative Medicine – guidelines to dosages for techniques that manifest results and maintain progress.

• Angel Notes – additional suggestions or applications for the use of a remedy.

To Receive the Best Results from a Remedy

The most important thing you can do before starting a technique is to relax and welcome Angelic support. Two exercises from the book, *Angel Love (Prosperity)* and *Breathing Technique (Career)* are recommended. Invite your favorite Angel Specialist to be with you while performing the remedies.

Additional Points to Remember

- Affirmations can enhance the effectiveness of Angelic remedies because they encourage belief in positive results. As declarative statements that focus on ideal situations, it is best to formulate affirmations in present tense and repeat them frequently. Begin with *"I am"* or *"I have."* It is especially beneficial to write or say these statements first thing in the morning and before going to sleep at night.

- Often in the remedies you are directed to invite, see or call upon the Angels to be present. Visualize them as being close by while following the exact instructions in the exercises. Believe in your heart that the Angels are there with you. This is the time to trust your faith. The techniques often use the words "request, tell or ask" referring to either silent or verbal communication with the Celestial Beings.

- Generate enthusiasm for the images in your visualizations and hold the positive feelings or sensations for at least one minute. When held in the body for this length of time, these emotions will be imprinted in your cells. After using an *Angel First Aid* Technique, loosen up by stretching your arms over your head.

- Practice the remedies when it is most convenient or comfortable for you. The instructions are guidelines. Do your best to follow the exercises as presented. Whenever necessary, use your own creativity to modify the suggested techniques.

- Take time to develop an ongoing relationship with your Angels. The more that communication with them becomes a natural part of your life, the easier it will be to enlist their support.

- Even though the Angels are involved, some remedies will take time to work. Be patient and persevere. If the intention is to improve your life, focus on that goal for success.

FREQUENTLY ASKED QUESTIONS ABOUT ANGELS

Why are there Angels?

Angels exist to provide protection, support, wisdom and unconditional love for everyone. Celestial Beings were created by God to make the lives of humans healthier, happier and more successful.

How are Angels involved in miracles?

People can view miracles in different ways. They often appear to be a coincidence, an unexpected event or an Angelic intervention. They are God's way of blessing us with many gifts. Angels hear a person's requests, deliver them to God, then carry out His wishes. Miracles happen to those who believe in miracles.

Are Angels accepted in every religion?

All the monotheistic religions of the world have acknowledged Angels as messengers of God. Throughout history, they have appeared in the writings and symbols of Christianity, Judaism, Islam, Buddhism and many other spiritual traditions. While the existence of Celestial Beings is accepted in most religions, it is not necessary to have a particular affiliation to enjoy their love, support and guidance.

What if a person does not believe in Angels?

Angels do God's work whether or not people believe in them. They have been created for this very purpose. The advantage of embracing the Angels is the uplifting feeling that comes from being the recipient of their love. Having a connection with the Celestial Beings gives a perpetual sense of guidance and support.

Are Angels all the same?

In the Angelic Realm, there is a hierarchy of Angels consisting of Archangels, Guardian Angels and Angel Specialists. Each has a particular area of expertise. Although the number of Guardian Angels is significant, the amount of Angel Specialists is infinite.

Who are the Archangels?

There are seven important and especially powerful Celestial Beings called "Archangels." Four of these attend to humanity. Archangel Michael, the Angel of Protection, oversees divine justice. Raphael, the Angel of Healing, promotes brotherhood. Uriel, the Angel of Spirituality, encourages prosperity. Gabriel, the Messenger Angel, works with communication and the arts.

How do Archangels and Guardian Angels differ?

Archangels have more involved responsibilities. They watch over a larger number of individuals, offering love and advice. Guardian Angels focus on the person they are assigned to help. All Celestial Beings will handle any situation in which support and protection are required. In addition, they provide peace, joy and friendship, allowing people to experience greater happiness.

Do people have more than one Guardian Angel?

Everyone has two Guardian Angels who work together as a team to assist in developing the unique gifts and talents that fulfill each individual's purpose. This is of double benefit to a person's life.

Why are there Angel Specialists?

God created Angel Specialists so that people could call upon the Angel most appropriate for the situation. These Celestial Beings have been given specific areas of expertise and are available to assist individuals in a variety of circumstances.

Can humans who have died become Angels?

People who are deceased can act as Angels for a period of time. They will often send a sign or symbol announcing their presence. Appearing as needed, these Angels leave after their missions have been accomplished.

In what ways can Angels help humanity?

Angels carry and deliver messages. No request is too large or too small for a Celestial Being's involvement. Angels do not need rest or sleep, therefore, they are available at any time. With their help, individuals can enjoy more fulfilling lives.

How are Angels assigned to people?

When people are born, three Angels are assigned to provide care and support. An Archangel and two Guardian Angels are chosen based on the individual's talents, gifts and life's purpose. Many other Celestial Beings are available for protection and guidance.

When do Angels appear?

Angels come when sent by God or if requested by individuals. Celestial Beings can make their presence known through sight, sound, touch or feelings. Some Angels can take on human form for a short period of time to serve a specific purpose. These Celestial Beings are usually referred to as "Physical Angels."

Do people pray to Angels?

Traditionally, people pray to God. He listens and responds by answering their requests. All miracles originate from Him. The Angels merely serve as the messengers of God's love, wisdom and blessings.

How do Angels make a difference in a person's life?

Angels can strengthen an individual's self-confidence. They are always at a person's side, ready to listen or offer advice. Celestial Beings take great delight in contributing to the miracles that make life more enjoyable. There is no limit to what they can do.

In what ways are Angels beneficial?

All areas of a person's life can improve with a connection to the Angels. Celestial Beings help in creating prosperity, success and well-being. Angels assist individuals in making their professional lives more rewarding and their personal lives more serene.

How can people learn the names of their Angels?

One of the best ways for individuals to identify their Archangel or Guardian Angel is to say aloud, *"Angel, what is your name?"* Then, listen for the response and trust the answer. If two names are heard, they both serve as the person's Angels.

Another method for finding the name of an Angel is to take the same question and write, *"Angel, what is your name?"* Celestial Beings will answer by helping the person write the correct name.

What is the best way to work with Angels?

When communicating with Angels, it is best to make detailed requests to let them know how they can be of assistance. The inclusion of Celestial Beings in a person's everyday activities establishes an interactive relationship.

Do Angels make contact in a specific way?

Angels will speak in any language that an individual understands. The messages are usually conveyed by the use of words, touch or visions. Frequently, a combination of these will be experienced.

How is an Angelic message recognized?

An individual realizes that a message comes from an Angel because of the warm, loving feeling that accompanies it. Often, practice is necessary to tell the difference between a person's thoughts and those from an Angelic source. However, once this skill has been mastered, communication flows freely.

What is the best way to speak to Angels?

A person can talk to Angels in the same way they speak to a dear friend. Sharing concerns, desires, ideas and accomplishments will strengthen the relationship. Inviting a Celestial Being to become an intimate and trusted confidante is especially rewarding.

Are Angels present at all times?

Angels are always available whether or not people communicate with them. The Celestial Beings are perpetually delivering God's miracles and providing love and guidance. They stay at a person's side for a lifetime, always ready to be of assistance.

What is the best way to receive Angelic guidance?

It is advisable to relax in peaceful, comfortable surroundings. A person benefits from being as specific as possible in formulating questions or requests in advance. When an individual listens and trusts, the answers flow. It is also beneficial to keep a journal of Angelic messages for future reference.

Is there a special time or place to contact the Angels?

Celestial Beings are available day or night. Interaction with them is best when a person is calm and peaceful. The Angels have an unlimited amount of time, are able to appear anywhere and love to be of service.

Do Angels have personalities?

All Angels are compassionate, understanding and have a sense of humor. Their distinct personalities are suited to the type of service they perform. For instance, Serena, the Angel of Children, can be playful and loves to have fun. Celestial Beings make wonderful, nurturing friends.

Are Angels ever jealous?

Jealousy does not exist in the Angelic Realm, so individuals can communicate and develop relationships with as many Celestial Beings as they desire. There is no competition between Angels.

Can Angels get upset?

Angels know only positive emotions such as peace and serenity. Celestial Beings are non-judgmental and caring. Their existence revolves around love and they want each person to share in this joyous experience.

Do pets have Guardian Angels?

Guardian Angels are assigned to pets based on the divine purpose of their owners. Animals provide unconditional love and support to people in the same way Angels bring happiness and security to the pet and its family.

How can Angels help the planet?

The Angels are doing everything possible to help the Earth and humanity. Celestial Beings can be instantly dispatched anywhere in the world. They assist in the improvement of the environment making the planet a better place to live. Angels also welcome the opportunity to participate in advancing world peace.

World Peace Angel ©

MIRACLE STORIES

The following are actual stories of people whose lives have been transformed by the love, insight and blessings of the Angels. In many of these cases, The Angel Lady's personal involvement was the catalyst between the Celestial Beings and the resulting miracles.

It is helpful to be aware of the various ways divine messages can be received and to recognize that assistance comes in many forms. Sometimes, Angels appear in our lives to provide encouragement and support. Under other circumstances, Celestial Beings are able to spark complete transformations. As individuals start to develop relationships with these incredible beings, all things are possible.

Angelic Melodies

Greg grew up in a very poor family living in the mountains of Tennessee. The typical childhood toys that most of us take for granted were not available to him. One of his few possessions was an old guitar, so he learned to play and compose songs as a hobby. Although Greg did not talk directly to the Angels, he connected with them through music. Years later, Greg told me that when he wrote lyrics, the words came to him as if Angels were whispering in his ear.

At a young age, Greg began to play for audiences, sharing his unique talent with more and more people. Supported by Perrie, the Angel of Music, he started writing compositions for famous country artists. Using his divine gifts, Greg became successful in a musical career with many of his songs making it to the top of the charts. He now works with struggling young artists encouraging them to listen to their Angels and follow the path to their dreams.

Angelic Encounter

While hearing me speak on a radio show, Eric called to share with the listeners a dramatic experience in which he came face-to-face with his Guardian Angel.

Eric was ten years old when this story took place. He began, "I went with my mother to pick up a carry-out lunch. She dropped me off at the restaurant, then drove across the street and waited. The line was longer than expected, making me late for my soccer game. When our order was ready, I bolted out the door and ran into the street. Suddenly, a strong force yanked me back towards the building just as a huge truck went speeding by. With my heart pounding, I looked up and was shocked to see a beautiful Angel! To this day, I don't fully understand what happened. However, the memory of my Guardian Angel still takes my breath away."

Eric's encounter reminded me of just how often Guardian Angels intervene to save a person's life. Protection is one of the greatest gifts provided by Celestial Beings.

Archangel's Appearance

When Jody called me, she sounded very excited about an incident that had just taken place involving her son, Andy. He was having trouble in his marriage and at work. Andy believed strongly in the Angels, but was starting to feel discouraged by life.

She began, "Andy was outside on the balcony, thinking over all his problems when Archangel Michael miraculously appeared in front of him. The Angel said, *Love the people who are in your life. Give them leeway to be human.* Hearing these words, Andy ran back into the apartment. Hardly able to speak and with a glow on his face, I had never seen him so happy."

Jody's call brightened my day. I knew that Archangel Michael's appearance could put a whole new perspective on Andy's future.

Physical Angel

At one of my workshops, Louise told the group about her white-water rafting adventure. Taking this kind of vacation seemed risky because she was not very athletic and had recently undergone hip surgery. Telling the story, Louise explained, "Midway through the trip, while in a narrow, turbulent part of the river, the raft tipped over. As the current pulled me under the murky water, I screamed for help from the Angels. At once, a Celestial Presence lifted me to the surface. Not yet out of danger, I repeated my plea and was guided to the side of the river. Exhausted, yet grateful to be alive, I still had a steep embankment in front of me to climb. Crying out again for the Angels, I felt my body being lifted by strong hands. They pushed me to the top of the ridge where a crowd of people had gathered.

"Immediately turning to thank my rescuer, I was surprised to see no one there. A young woman, watching from a distance, ran over to check if I was hurt and needed help. She said that a man riding a motorcycle stopped, jumped off, slid down the cliff and waited by the riverbank. Then he pushed me up here and disappeared."

After Louise finished telling the story about her incredible rescue, I explained to the audience that the man on the motorcycle was a perfect example of a "Physical Angel."

How Angels Work

Three years ago, Stacy came to see me for an Angelic consultation. Extremely unhappy with her boss, she had been contemplating early retirement. Stacy was already communicating with the Angels. However, she felt the need for additional information from Archangel Michael. He advised waiting for six more months before considering leaving her present job.

Shortly after this suggested time frame, Stacy called and said, "I've been telling everyone. It happened just the way Archangel Michael had said it would. At exactly six months, my boss got a promotion to another position. My new manager is wonderful! We get along very well. I am so glad that I waited and took Archangel Michael's advice."

A great feeling of excitement came over me hearing Stacy relate her experience. My response to her was, "This is the way Angels work – everyone benefits."

Guardian Angels

At one of my lectures, a woman named Jan shared her Angelic miracles with the audience. She said, "My eighteen-year-old son, Don, was riding his new motorcycle through a hilly section of a national park. After hitting a bump, his glasses fell off. He found them, but the lenses were cracked. Unable to see the path clearly, Don rode the motorcycle over a steep ridge, falling sixteen feet. He was not seriously injured and walked to safety. Don told me it felt as though his body had been gently lowered to the ground.

"A tiny female Angel, who I named Lily, appeared in my field of vision at the same time the park ranger contacted me. I knew right away that it was Lily who had saved Don. This Angel is still with me and has become a welcome part of my life.

"Weeks later, I was driving Don and his friend to a baseball game. When we came to a stop at a three-way intersection, I felt Lily's presence and pressure against my shoulders. She was holding me back in the seat so that I could not move. At the same moment, a red van flew through the stop sign. Once again, Lily had come to our family's rescue."

How lucky Jan is to have this special Angel with her at all times. Lily is a constant reminder of celestial support and protection.

Winning with Angels

After serving on the school board for many years and developing a keen interest in improving education, Laura decided to run for the state legislature. All odds were against her. Laura's opponents had strong financial backing and were much better known in the community. In fact, months before the election, a poll showed that less than one-third of all the voters even recognized Laura's name. However, consulting with Jacob, the Angel of Education, she was confident of winning.

So, we each did our part. My role was to show Laura how to use visualization to her benefit. Picturing every detail of the election including the victory celebration was first. Next, we concentrated on eliminating blocks to success. I also placed Laura's campaign buttons and posters in my office, finding opportunities to connect with the Angels on her behalf. It worked! Laura's victory was a miracle! Along with Jacob and other Angels, she now holds a seat in the state legislature.

Angel Dolls

Margo, in her fifties, divorced and the mother of grown children, was concerned about keeping the small, cozy home that she loved. Through no fault of her own, Margo had lost five jobs in the last several years. Frequently speaking to the Angels, Margo asked, "How can I make my life better?" The Angels heard her question and, with their blessings, Margo began to live by a "new rule." In her words, *"No matter what happens to me, I will always be happy."*

As a hobby, Margo made Angel dolls. A close friend suggested that she develop her talent into a career. With the Angels' help, Margo's business has become a success. Following the path to happiness, Margo met Ted, her soul mate. Now married, they own a large new home, travel extensively across the country and are experiencing great joy.

There was so much wisdom in Margo's decision that I often use her story in my presentations. Choosing to be happy is a rule that anyone can live by.

Angelic Intervention

Kathleen, a stay-at-home mom, was widowed in her early forties. She had been left with four children to raise and very little money.

This is Kathleen's story. "An Angel appeared in a dream and told me to become a nurse. Following his advice led to a satisfying career, but I still had difficulty supporting my family. So I asked the Angels for another source of income. In a second dream, the same Angel showed me a book about visualization. I found it on a shelf at the library. A technique of repeatedly picturing a desired amount of money caught my attention. I chose $400,000 – which represented $100,000 for each of my children. A miracle occurred a year later when a man hired to search for missing heirs called. He said that an uncle had left me an estate of exactly $400,000!"

It is amazing how precise Angels can be when matching numbers with desires. They act as a bridge between our dreams and reality.

Protected by Angels

Once when I was on a popular radio talk show, the host asked listeners to call in with their stories about Guardian Angels. The switchboard lit up! Every person's encounter had a similar theme. Terri, a magazine photographer, was the first one to get through. She explained that during a routine trip to buy film, an astounding incident occurred. In her words, "While driving at a steady clip on a busy street, I heard a loud, male voice screaming, *Stop the car!* Although the traffic signal was still green and there were no other vehicles in sight, I slammed on the brakes and screeched to a halt. At the same instant, two cars, drag-racing, ran the red light. I am convinced that my Guardian Angel saved my life."

Stories like Terri's show that people who have experienced this kind of encounter develop a lasting closeness with their Angels.

PROSPERITY

How Angel First Aid Helps You Develop Prosperity

Prosperity is more than the attainment of wealth or money. It is truly a joyous way of living. This rich and fulfilling state of being is experienced when every aspect of a person's life is in balance. With assistance from the Angels, people can achieve and enjoy the wholeness, love, inner peace and financial security that signify a prosperous life.

Angel First Aid for Prosperity provides you with ways to tap into the unending flow of divine resources that are readily available.

Angel Specialists

Archangel Uriel

Barry	Angel of Strength
Bettina	Angel of Creativity
Evelyn	Angel of Manifesting
Katrina	Angel of Prosperity
Lucien	Angel of Resources
Robert	Angel of Balance
Ruth	Angel of Divine Justice
Tara	Angel of Love
Timothy	Angel of Good Fortune

Affirmations

I am prosperous now.

I have all that is desired.

I am happy and calm.

I am loved and appreciated.

I have an abundant life.

Case Study

Lisa, a bright woman in her thirties, could not put down roots or advance financially. She desperately wanted more stability in life. Lisa's goal was to buy a new home. Unfortunately, she had lost her job, making it impossible to qualify for a mortgage.

There were so many things in my life that appeared to be broken. After hearing about Angel First Aid, I began using Stacking Cash. In this visualization, Timothy, the Angel of Good Fortune, brought me handfuls of money. A few days later, a distant relative offered the funds needed for a down payment and I was able to obtain a bank loan.

Still unemployed, I began to use Golden Cylinder and Prosperity Painting to bring financial security into my life. Wanting to rejoin the workforce, I accepted a temp job as a receptionist. Executives who noticed my talents invested more than ten thousand dollars in training me. Today I am making a six-figure income heading up a product management group. After my financial house was in order, something incredible and unexpected happened. James, my boyfriend, started to use Angel First Aid Techniques, especially the Expanding Heart exercise. Six weeks later, he proposed. I am now happily married, have a successful career and enjoy living in the house purchased with the blessings of the Angels. Life is good!

Remedies

Angel Love

Feel complete after using this remedy.
It allows you to experience a sense of
well-being and a pipeline to unlimited
resources. Begin by filling your heart
with love. Savor this feeling. Connect
the love in your heart with the love of
your spirit. Then, add the love of your
soul. Enjoy the peace that envelops you. Bring in the love of God.
You are now totally balanced and immersed in love. Use this time
to think, meditate, visualize or speak to the Angels. If searching
for your life's purpose, pray for guidance and listen carefully for
the answer to come to you. Invite the Angels to participate in your
quest for harmony and serenity.

Dosage: Daily, or as desired

Time Prosperity

To increase the amount of time you have, take advantage of what
is known as "Angelic Time." Try practicing this remedy to attain
a higher level of productivity. Begin by imagining that your chest
is expanded an additional six inches to either side. Visualize your
upper body remaining in this state, filled with the extra space. Go
about performing the activities for which the extension in time is
necessary. Return your chest to its original size when the exercise
is completed. This technique is invaluable for creating a sense of
security and additional peace of mind.

Dosage: As needed

The Judge

Releasing self-sabotaging habits is very important for achieving success. The cause is negative self-talk. The perpetrator is called "the Judge." To begin eliminating the Judge, visualize his image. Next, construct a representation of him with pencil, crayons or modeling clay. In order to defuse the Judge, recognize the signs that indicate his presence, such as the recollection of criticizing or disempowering messages first heard in childhood. These early thoughts are always accompanied by physical discomfort or a gut feeling that you have done something wrong. The Judge is most likely to strike when a person is stressed, so ask Archangel Uriel to keep you calm. Practice the *Breathing Technique (Career)* and remain as peaceful as possible. Repeat some of the affirmations listed at the beginning of this chapter. Finally, ask the Angels to remind you of your best qualities. Focus on these attributes for at least five minutes each day.

Dosage: Once a month, or when feeling down

Backbone

Material wealth and richness of experience come to all individuals who act self-assured. Appear more powerful and command respect by moving energy from the front of your body into your backbone. Next, call upon Barry, the Angel of Strength, to direct attention to your spine. Concentrate on this area for one minute. The stronger you become, the easier it is to move forward on a path to creating prosperity in your life.

Dosage: Two times a day, or as necessary

Angel Notes: This technique will help you set boundaries and stand your ground. It can easily be applied to any situation in which more strength or courage is needed.

Golden Cylinder

Successful endeavors in your personal and professional lives are derived from Angelic partnerships. To feel the strength and power of these connections, imagine a golden cylinder that extends from the crown of your head to the Angelic Realm. This cylinder opens a direct channel to enable the continuous flow of prosperity. Ask Lucien, the Angel of Resources, to polish it to a radiant sheen. He brings blessings of abundance into your life. Picture the cylinder remaining in place for at least one minute. There is a cumulative effect in performing this remedy. For the best results, repeat the exercise often.

Dosage: Once a day

Prosperity Painting

The ability to manifest prosperity will increase when the Angels assist with this remedy. Visualize standing in front of a white wall. Working with paints, begin creating a mural depicting abundance in all forms. Actually see yourself holding the brush and making the movements. Be sure to include the Angels and anyone else who can offer support. Focus on your excitement as the painting begins to take shape. Imagine living happily in this scene. Artistic talent is not necessary – the picture will appear exactly as you see it. Signing your name clearly, call upon Bettina, the Angel of Creativity, to take it with her up to the Angelic Realm. Here the Angels frame your painting of prosperity and make it into a glorious reality for the future.

Dosage: As desired

Colors of Balance

Angels see various aspects of human energy as colors. Physical well-being is pink, mental clarity is yellow, emotional stability is sky blue and spiritual enlightenment is lavender. Prosperity can be experienced when a person's colors are in balance. To accomplish this, begin visualizing four bricks: one each of pink, yellow, blue and lavender. Nearby is the Statue of Justice holding a scale in her right hand. Robert, the Angel of Balance, observes as you place the pink and blue bricks on one side of the scale and the yellow and lavender bricks on the other. Remain quiet for one minute, enjoying the calming effect that comes from being in a state of perfect balance.

Dosage: Once a day, in the morning

Angel Notes: When desiring an interaction with another person to become more harmonious, you can use a modified version of the Colors of Balance technique. Visualize the individual holding a scale with the four colored bricks lined up as described in the above remedy. Retain the image for one minute. Using this new version can be especially helpful for people who have Attention Deficit Disorder, dyslexia or other types of learning disabilities.

Merry-Go-Round

To be prosperous and gain more personal power, use this exercise. See yourself sitting on a bench in the center of a merry-go-round. Barry, the Angel of Strength, is at your side for support. Riding the horses of the carousel are people who represent situations in your life that need healing. Next to you is an empty basket with a handle. Pick it up, then with the Angel, approach each person on the merry-go-round. Imagine all these people returning what they have taken from you. This is the perfect opportunity to retrieve your dignity, confidence, self-respect or other attributes. Handing the basket to Barry, visualize him holding it above your head. As he empties the contents into your body, follow the energy down to your navel where it will remain. Take a deep breath, noticing how complete you feel. Envision the individuals on the carousel either fading away or changing into loving and supportive people. Now, return to the bench and sit for at least one minute while enjoying the feeling of contentment. Leave, knowing the wholeness and comfort you have just experienced will lead to greater prosperity.

Dosage: Once a week, or when needed

Preventative Medicine:

Two remedies, two times per week
Three affirmations, three times a week

Light of the Universe©

RELATIONSHIPS

How Angel First Aid Helps Improve Relationships

Relationships are interactions between individuals that are meant to bring great joy and accelerate personal growth. Angels can be instrumental in deepening bonds between people. Celestial Beings act as matchmakers pairing soul mates or finding companions. While promoting balance and harmony, Angels also enhance communication. Watching people have fun with their loved ones is one of the activities the Angels like best!

Angel First Aid for Relationships allows you to develop more rewarding and lasting personal associations.

Angel Specialists

Archangel Michael

Eileen	Angel of Happiness
Kevin	Angel of Friendship
Melody	Angel of Self-Esteem
Robin	Angel of Social Contact
Sarah	Angel of Harmony
Serena	Angel of Children
Tara	Angel of Love
Terina	Angel of Attraction

Affirmations

I have healthy, loving relationships.

I am a whole and complete person.

I am accepting love each day.

I am attracting my soul mate.

I have many wonderful friends.

I am bringing helpful people my way.

I have harmonious relationships.

Case Study

After having spent many years in an unhappy marriage, Jean was recently divorced. The mother of three teenagers, she worked as a freelance journalist for a major newspaper.

During my lengthy marriage, money had always been a big issue. My ex-husband and I never seemed to get along or see eye-to-eye. After hearing about Angel First Aid Techniques, I practiced the remedies relating to Careers and Business. I had great hope for financial independence. The Angels provided tremendous support because, after nine months, my annual income jumped from only $6,000 to $40,000.

With newfound energy and enthusiasm, it was now time to find my soul mate. I began exploring remedies for creating romance in a healthy relationship. Selecting Likes Attract, Statement for Love and Blue Sphere techniques, it was my intention to bring someone special into my life. Requesting that the Angels arrange for me to meet an ideal partner was a daily ritual.

Within months, I met a man who was loving and prosperous. We married and are now living a wonderful life. Still communicating with my Angels, I am looking forward to future miracles.

Remedies

Expanding Heart

The ability to give and accept love can be
developed through the use of this exercise.
With your index finger, draw a small heart
in the air in front of you. Continue drawing
larger and larger hearts, involving your whole
body in the motion. Repeat the entire process
three times, always starting with a small heart.
Focus attention on the euphoric feeling that is
growing within. By holding the memory of this wonderful moment
for one minute, you will become more open to love. Trust that the
Angels are creating happiness for your future.

Dosage: As desired

Statement for Love

Angels and people can team up to expand love and other positive
aspects of a relationship. To begin the remedy, use the following
affirmation. Add the particulars that relate to the situation, *"The
relationship that I have with my (significant other, mother, father,
child, friend) is one that accelerates our happiness and growth.
Each of us is rewarded with love, harmony and stability."* Repeat
the statement three times. This exercise is especially effective for
releasing past differences or taking a relationship to a deeper level.

Dosage: Daily, before bed

Likes Attract

To develop a healthy, loving relationship with someone new, ask Archangel Michael to assist by activating the **Law of Attraction.**

This is how it works: *"Like attracts like."* As a mirror reflects an image, the qualities and values that you will attract in a mate are similar to those you already possess. If an attribute in a person is appealing, check to see if that same particular trait is one of your own strong points. Be honest and non-judgmental with yourself. Is improvement necessary in any of the following areas: attitude, health or financial stability? Consider if you need more patience, compassion or loyalty. Practicing *Angel First Aid* remedies helps develop these characteristics. It is advantageous to write or affirm three times, *"I am invoking the Law of Attraction."*

Request that the Celestial Beings provide their assistance in the search for your heart's desire. Anything is possible when working together with the Angels.

Dosage: As needed

Blue Sphere

The Angels love to see people enjoying life with their soul mates. This visualization will begin that process. Imagine the person you intend to attract seated in a large blue sphere. Include all desirable characteristics, being sure to add height, weight, attitude, lifestyle and talents. Continue to fill the blue sphere with the special values and qualities you seek in another person. Think how wonderful it will be to share a relationship with your soul mate. Maintain this excitement for one minute, then see the Angels coming to carry the sphere back to the Angelic Realm. Request that the Celestial Beings find the ideal person to fill your life and arrange for you to meet.

Dosage: Daily

Angel Notes: *This technique can be adapted to attain a more meaningful life. Place your own image in the blue sphere and add the qualities you wish to gain. Then, relax and enjoy the beneficial results.*

Enhancing Relationships

To enhance an existing relationship, envision painting a picture of the most favorable situation imaginable. Include all the particulars. (How are the two of you spending time together?) Be sure to add sounds, such as music and laughter, to increase the feeling of joy in this scene. Think about the happiness and comfort you provide for each other, relating in this new way. Infuse the painting with lavender light to solidify your vision. Then, frame the picture in a decorative manner. Ask the Angels to create the perfect relationship for you and your partner.

Dosage: Three times a week

Forgiveness

To have a healthy relationship that is of mutual benefit, utilize this exercise. Request that Archangel Michael be at your side. Imagine the other person standing in front of you. Then, say, _"Forgive me for anything that I have knowingly or unknowingly done to hurt you."_ Now, taking a deep breath, add, _"I forgive you for anything that you have knowingly or unknowingly done to hurt me."_ Know that forgiveness does not condone an individual's behavior. It will simply allow you to move on with your life. Savor this newfound freedom. The path is now clear to receiving all the blessings from the Angelic Realm.

Dosage: Repeat, at least once a day

Preventative Medicine

Two remedies, three times a week
Two affirmations, two times a week

Sleeping Cherub©

MONEY

How Angel First Aid Helps You Attract and Enjoy Money

Money provides the ability to achieve a more comfortable lifestyle. Supported by Angels, individuals can become prosperous and experience greater abundance. Financial security allows for monetary independence and provides peace of mind. When people are on a path to creating wealth, collaborating with Angels increases the potential to be successful and fulfilled.

Angel First Aid for Money helps in acquiring the funds that allow you to enjoy a more rewarding and affluent life.

Angel Specialists

Archangel Gabriel

Alan	Angel of Investments
Evelyn	Angel of Manifesting
Jeremiah	Angel of Financial Security
Katrina	Angel of Prosperity
Loretta	Angel of New Enterprise
Lucien	Angel of Resources
Nancy	Angel of Productivity
Timothy	Angel of Good Fortune
Trevor	Angel of Stocks

Affirmations

I am a mighty money magnet.

I have financial security.

I am enjoying being wealthy.

I have plenty of cash available.

I have an abundance of money.

I am happy and prosperous.

Case Study

Peggy, a woman in her thirties, was making $28,000 a year as an administrative assistant in a large corporation. While she held a master's degree, her job and salary did not reflect that high level of education.

Trying to understand why my income was so low, I began working with the Money Memory technique to identify my first thoughts of money. I remembered that when I was eight years old my mother said, "A woman cannot earn over $30,000 a year." Realizing this misconception was keeping me from success, I tried practicing the Play Money, Stacking Cash and Dollar Sign exercises. To become more comfortable with the idea of earning larger sums of money, every day I wrote several affirmations. Two of my favorites were "I am a mighty money magnet" and "I have financial security."

Three months after starting Angel First Aid for Money techniques, a promotion and raise boosted my annual income to $35,000. The early indoctrination of believing that I could not earn more than $30,000 a year had been shattered.

Next, I worked with Angel First Aid for Career and Business. Six weeks later, after landing a new job in the insurance industry, I was offered a starting salary of $65,000. Now, accepting a job transfer to another city, my income will increase again.

Remedies

True Money Beliefs

Angels want you to have a positive
and natural relationship with money.
However, the potential for wealth can be
sabotaged by holding on to limiting beliefs.
For example, people use expressions such as
"money doesn't grow on trees" or "easy come,
easy go." The Angels will help release these ideas.
To speed up the process, perform this exercise. Write down all the
misleading messages you have ever heard about money on a piece
of paper. When finished, tear the page into shreds. Now, throw it
away. Feel a sense of freedom growing inside. Next, select several
affirmations from the beginning of this chapter and read, write or
say them out loud three times. This reinforces your new positive
attitude towards money.

Dosage: When needed

Money Memory

To improve your relationship with money, start by replacing early
misconceptions. For example, Tina remembered asking her father
for a dollar when she was seven years old. He responded abruptly
by slapping her. Tina grew up afraid to ask for money. Years later,
she realized this was damaging her real estate career. Negotiating
a sales contract was difficult, if not impossible. After pinpointing
the childhood memory and reversing it through the use of verbal
affirmations, Tina became successful in closing deals. Consider if
you, too, can profit from using the following remedy.

Begin this technique by calling upon the Angels. Place one hand on your forehead and the other hand over the back of your head between the ears. Remembering the first contact you had with money, attempt to recall, in detail, the feelings present at the time. This is very important, so clear your mind and concentrate. Think about whether these ideas are reflected in your

current financial situation. Are there any circumstances that you would like to change? What new concepts need to be created to support a more comfortable lifestyle? When finished, lower your hands. Then, choose three affirmations from the beginning of this chapter. Repeat them several times each day. Now, with Angelic advice, develop a plan to integrate these new, prosperous beliefs.

Dosage: Whenever needed

Plug Money Leaks

If your expenses are greater than you would like, use this remedy. Visualize a bathtub full of cash. Jeremiah, the Angel of Financial Security, and six Cherubs are standing close by to stop the money from "going down the drain." Imagine Jeremiah placing a large plug into the bathtub. Now, celebrate – the leak has been stopped! Breathe a sigh of relief and allow the scene to slowly fade away. Next, envision a beautiful fountain shooting streams of water high into the air. The Angels reappear to enjoy the arc of the spray. This flowing water, which symbolizes your money supply, is constantly being replenished. Focus on building a nest egg and ask Jeremiah to join in as you say, *"A major part of all I have is mine to keep."* The Angels and Cherubs will gladly help you create abundance.

Dosage: Daily, or as often as necessary

Stacking Cash

The Angels know that people can only manifest as much money as their minds and bodies can accept. This exercise prepares you to feel comfortable with abundance. Imagine Timothy, the Angel of Good Fortune, giving you handfuls of money. Each piece of currency is a $50 or $100 bill. Start stacking the bills next to you. Reach out for more. Every time your hands are extended, Timothy quickly replenishes the supply. When the cash is overflowing, the Angel offers a key that opens a special safe in the center of your body. Put the money there so it can grow. Feel excited about the prospect of building your fortune. Using this remedy is helpful to nurturing a close relationship with Timothy. Offer him thanks for handing you the key to abundant riches.

Dosage: Daily

Plenty Exercise

To ensure a sufficient supply of whatever you desire in your life, concentrate on the word *"PLENTY."* Think of it in the context of all that is important to you. There is plenty of money, happiness, love and time. Say the word out loud – *"Plenty, Plenty, Plenty."* Write it on an unlined piece of paper seventeen times every day. Have fun with this technique and believe that, through Angelic blessings and miracles, plenty is in your future.

Dosage: Four times a day

Angel Notes: Be creative with "Plenty" by including the word often in thoughts and conversations. The benefits of performing this exercise are cumulative and provide additional prosperity.

Play Money

Possessing material wealth brings a strong sense of freedom and enthusiasm. When you become accustomed to having money in large denominations, greater amounts of cash will enter your life. Being comfortable with handling money tells the Celestial Beings to increase your financial blessings. Start by carrying play money. The Game of Life® has $100,000 bills. Each time you see or touch the "pretend cash," it demonstrates to the Angels your willingness to accept more abundance.

Dosage: Whenever cash is desired

Money, Money Everywhere

Allow the Angels to elevate your level of prosperity. Become accustomed to seeing money in familiar places. Using at least twenty one-dollar bills, take two or more singles and fold them together. Place these rolls of cash in drawers, pockets, cabinets, cars or anywhere they will be noticed every day. Each time you find some of this "stash," think of how your money is growing.

Dosage: As needed

Money Smiles

Draw or place a smiley face on everything that is associated with money and abundance – checkbooks, portfolio statements or other relevant documents. Smiles signal the Angels that you are happy with money and want them to increase your supply. For additional prosperity, you may want to keep a smile on your face, too.

Dosage: As often as necessary

Dollar Sign

To increase the amount of "fast cash" available, perform the following. Using your index finger, draw small dollar signs directly in front of you. Continue drawing them larger and larger, using your whole body as part of the motion. Repeat the remedy three times, always starting with a small dollar sign. The Angels will respond by helping to manifest greater amounts of money.

Dosage: Three times a day

Wealth Affirmation

Invite Katrina, the Angel of Prosperity, to help you in establishing a continuous supply of material abundance. Utilize the following technique. While tapping gently on each of your temples, say this statement, *"I give myself permission to receive wealth."* Repeat it five times. Katrina will carry your prosperity affirmation with her to the Angelic Realm where Angels will work to hasten the flow of money coming in your direction.

Dosage: Daily

Preventative Medicine:

Two remedies, three times a week
Two affirmations, two times a week

HEALTH

How Angel First Aid Helps You Achieve Health

Optimal health allows a person's life to be filled with pep and vitality. People who have good health feel youthful and enthusiastic. When a person's mind, body and spirit are in harmony, it is easy to create success and to enjoy a greater sense of prosperity. With the help of the Angels, everyone can be energetic and approach life with zest.

Angel First Aid for Health includes remedies to assist in building a strong, vigorous body while maintaining a sense of well-being.

Angel Specialists

Archangel Raphael

Barry	Angel of Strength
Blake	Angel of Comfort
Eileen	Angel of Happiness
Florence	Angel of Compassion
Gunther	Angel of Fitness
Mirra	Angel of Healing Arts
Peter	Angel of Health
Robert	Angel of Balance
Solomon	Angel of Security

Affirmations

I am happy and healthy.

I have a positive attitude.

I have a strong mind and body.

I am always in present time.

I have excellent health.

I have a choice in what I do.

I am feeling energetic.

I have a zest for life.

Case Study

Diane, a woman of fifty, suffered from health problems related to having contracted polio as a child. She described her symptoms as debilitating headaches, vertigo, muscle spasms and lack of energy. Due to her severe handicap, Diane barely had enough mobility to maintain a career.

Using the Wastebasket exercise, I released troubling memories of having been a helpless child in the hospital. The Vitality Plus and Medium Blue techniques began restoring my health. A week later, the headaches were gone and there was a dramatic increase in my energy level. Suddenly, life seemed worth living again.

Once my health started to improve, I began to use Angel First Aid Techniques to make a major career change. Angel Scrapbook and several other visualizations helped clarify my goals and gave me self-confidence. I realized, after deep soul searching, that helping people with the same condition was my life's work. At the present time, I am working for a social service agency, creating a support program for people affected with post-polio syndrome. The future looks exciting and much more promising.

Remedies

Energy Tap

Ask for Angelic blessings as you perform the following movements. This exercise will help increase the flow of energy and enhance your sense of well-being. Place one hand over your navel. Take the other hand and gently tap each of these areas at 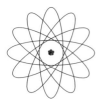 least ten times: below the bottom of your collar bones where they connect to the breastbone; above the upper lip and just below the lower lip; over the tailbone and on the crown of the head. Then, switch hands and repeat the exercise. Use *Energy Tap* often as an effective "pick-me-up" remedy.

Dosage: Daily

Vitality Plus

With the Angels nearby, perform this exercise to spark enthusiasm and generate good health. For added benefit, use it if you want to lose weight. Place your non-dominant hand on your throat. Now, let the other arm drop to your side. With the index finger pointed towards the floor, begin spinning the wrist quickly in a clockwise circle while counting to forty. For balanced metabolism, weight loss and a general lift, continue to use the remedy several times each day.

Dosage: As needed

Healthy Body

This exercise imprints in your cells a desire for vibrant health and energy. Imagine Archangel Raphael standing close by. To start the exercise, close your eyes, then use the fingertips of each hand to rub the temples in a circular motion. Place your fingertips in the center of each temple, moving them forward and down. Say out loud, _"I have a harmonious relationship with my healthy body."_ Repeat this affirmation together with the circular motion at least five times. Then, open your eyes and perform the same exercise twice more.

Dosage: Daily, or as needed

Power of Eight

If you are experiencing discomfort in some part of your body, do the following. Relax and use the _Breathing Technique (Career)_. Then, put your index finger over the place which needs healing and begin to make a _Figure Eight_ five times. When starting to draw, imagine the Angels infusing the area with lavender light to bring additional relief.

Dosage: Repeat often

Medium Blue

To restore energy and a feeling of balance, ask the Angels to use medium blue, their favorite color for healing. Visualize Peter, the Angel of Health, appearing to "take you under his wing." While enfolded in Angel love, he infuses your body with medium blue. It fills your heart, then flows in every direction until each cell is saturated. Keep the special color in your body as long as needed. By utilizing this remedy, it will be easier for Peter to carry out his Angelic healing work.

Dosage: Three times a week

Wastebasket

For creating more vibrant health, envision Florence, the Angel of Compassion, standing nearby for support. After placing one hand over your forehead, the other on the back of your head, recall the experiences that have been the most stressful or problematic since childhood. Now, imagine tossing into a large wastebasket all the thoughts and feelings associated with these memories. Enhance this technique by using hand motions that mimic throwing away crumpled pieces of paper. Florence is smiling and caring for you as the unpleasant experiences are being released. Let them leave and be gone forever. Then, lower your hands, becoming aware of how relieved and energized you feel. As Florence takes away the wastebasket, she bestows her blessings for future happiness.

Dosage: Whenever necessary

Picture of Health

To experience optimal health and accept healing from the Angelic Realm, imagine yourself having fun participating in activities that interest you. Visualize taking a vacation, playing a sport or going to the theater. Invite the Angels to help generate enthusiasm for a healthier way to live and bring it into reality. Notice that you are beginning to feel better. Then, thank the Angels for their uplifting and generous support.

Dosage: As needed

Preventative Medicine:

Two remedies, three times a week
Two affirmations, two times a week

HAPPINESS

How Angel First Aid Helps You to Achieve Happiness

Angels can serve as loving partners in assisting people to experience happiness as a state of mind. When a person shares a connection with Angels, having fun becomes an everyday occurrence. The Celestial Beings encourage individuals to follow their bliss and are delighted to be involved at all times.

Angel First Aid for Happiness helps you fill your days with joy, enthusiasm and prosperity.

Angel Specialists

Archangel Michael

Caroline	Angel of Positive Thinking
Eileen	Angel of Happiness
Joseph	Angel of Joy
Lorena	Angel of Divine Grace
Marilyn	Angel of Leisure
Rachel	Angel of Inspiration
Sarah	Angel of Harmony
Solomon	Angel of Security
Tara	Angel of Love
William	Angel of Peace

Affirmations

I have happiness in my life.

I am loved by the Angels.

I am whole and complete.

I have inner peace.

I am enjoying prosperity.

I am attracting love.

I have fun with my friends.

I am smiling all the time.

I am excited about life.

Case Study

Judy was a self-employed woman in her early forties. Although she was not faced with any serious difficulties, life seemed boring and uneventful. Judy's close friends noticed that she seldom smiled. It appeared that happiness had eluded her.

In a second marriage, without children to raise, my life had become ordinary and routine. Each day, I just went through the motions of existence until my best friend introduced me to Angel First Aid. In an effort to find happiness, I began to practice the techniques with enthusiasm. The Sack of Gold remedy helped me to identify what I treasured in life. Filling the bag with love, peace and wisdom made every day more enjoyable. Then came the Smiley Balloon exercise for increasing my self-confidence. As these remedies took effect, my optimism grew and I wanted to keep right on going. Next, I selected techniques from Angel First Aid for Inner Peace and Relationships. The results were truly remarkable! As I continue on a spiritual path and enjoy a new outlook, my marriage and friendships have really blossomed. Life has changed for the better.

Remedies

Forest Stream

To feel the continual flow of love, visualize being seated by a forest stream, enjoying the serenity of nature. Flowers are blooming in the sunshine. Eileen, the Angel of Happiness, appears as a vision, looking very beautiful in a pink gown. She showers you with blessings. Your heart begins to respond by opening up to her unconditional love. Feel warmth and peace coming into your body, permeating every cell. Hold this sensation for at least one minute. When the visualization is completed, Eileen departs with an approving smile on her face. This experience and the euphoric feeling that comes with it can be recreated at any time by saying the words "Angel Love."

Dosage: Daily

Body Laugh

Laugh and have fun with your Angels. Remember something you heard or saw that was really funny. Now, laugh. Just laugh, laugh, laugh. Laugh from head to toe. Notice how your chest loosens up, creating an expanded area that can be filled with Angelic love and blessings. Using this remedy will make room for more merriment in your life.

Dosage: Three times a week, or as desired

Twisting

To generate enthusiasm and a zest for life, perform the following exercise for fun. Stretch your arms out to the side, keeping them at shoulder level. Now, start twisting at the waist while swinging your arms rhythmically from side to side. Invite the Angels to join in. They imitate the motion by using their wings. Celestial Beings do not tire, so twist as long as you like. Enjoy doing this exercise to music while smiling and thinking happy thoughts. For the best results, use the remedy at least two minutes at a time.

Dosage: Whenever you need a boost

Voice Mail

To ensure greater happiness, imagine that you are in constant communication with your Angels. All their messages are being recorded on Celestial voice mail. At least once a day, check to see if they have left any words of wisdom. Enjoy receiving the warm, loving feeling that comes over you while listening to the Angelic messages.

Dosage: Once a day, or as desired

Sack of Gold

This is a wonderful exercise for quickly manifesting happiness. To fill every day with experiences that will bring great joy, perform this remedy. Picture a velvet sack attached to an imaginary belt around your waist. Feel excitement as you begin using this technique.

Visualize gathering and placing into the sack several objects that have special meaning to you. Be creative. Imagine taking a piece of the sky, water from a lake, branches of a tree or some fresh-cut flowers. Add intangibles such as love, joy, peace and knowledge. Rachel, the Angel of Inspiration, is available to help you choose items for your collection. Look for additional treasures throughout the day. Have fun with this remedy. It brings powerful energy into your life.

Dosage: Daily

Smiley Balloon

To feel more worthwhile and self-confident, utilize this technique. Picture a seven-foot-high yellow smiley face balloon. Look for a door around the back. Open it and walk inside. Angels with happy smiling faces greet you. Accept their invitation to make yourself comfortable. Now, begin by recalling all of the achievements that have brought you good feelings. Let the Celestial Beings express approval for your accomplishments. Admiring looks are reflected on their Angelic faces. Stay in the balloon for at least one minute. When it is time to leave, close the door while savoring the boost to your self-esteem.

Dosage: Three times a week

Preventative Medicine:

Two remedies, two times a week
One affirmation, three times a week

INNER PEACE

How Angel First Aid Helps You to Achieve Inner Peace

Angels can be tremendous assets in your quest for inner peace. Serving as God's messengers, they continually deliver His blessings of love and support. Inner peace bolsters an individual's belief that all is well and that there is an infinite amount of hope. When people experience this sense of connection, it enhances their ability to feel whole and complete.

Angel First Aid for Inner Peace strengthens your relationship with the Angels and leads to a life of joy and contentment.

Angel Specialists

Archangel Uriel

Joseph	Angel of Joy
Katrina	Angel of Prosperity
Lorena	Angel of Divine Grace
Rachel	Angel of Inspiration
Robert	Angel of Balance
Sarah	Angel of Harmony
Serena	Angel of Children
Tara	Angel of Love
William	Angel of Peace

Affirmations

I am filled with Angel love.

I am experiencing inner peace.

I have serenity in my life.

I am surrounded by blessings.

I am calm and balanced.

I have great inner strength.

I am happy and content.

Case Study

Single and in his mid-forties, Bill was employed as a high school principal. He felt lonely, restless and disconnected. For years, Bill had longed for inner peace and a loving relationship. He also had a vision of some day giving motivational seminars.

I learned about Angel First Aid Techniques and began practicing the Golden Temple and Moonlit Night. These remedies helped me to become more comfortable with myself. Angelic Adventure was beneficial in developing a deeper bond with the Angels. Enjoying a better relationship with them brought me peace.

I decided to try other Angel First Aid remedies to clear the path for attracting a romantic relationship into my life. Blue Sphere made me think about all the qualities I wanted in a partner. Five weeks later, I met and began dating Carrie. She turned out to be my soul mate. The next option was to look at career techniques that would enable me to fulfill my vision of facilitating seminars.

Carrie and I are now happily married and travel together giving motivational workshops on spirituality. Inner peace has become a part of our lives.

Remedies

Serena's Embrace

Use this visualization for creating inner peace. Close your eyes and allow Serena, the Guardian Angel of Children, to wrap her large, white wings around you. Enjoy the all-encompassing warmth of being in an Angel's embrace. Hold the feeling for at least one minute. As Serena opens her wings, she whispers this message in your ear, "To experience love and peace at any time, simply recall this moment of bliss. Trust that I will always be with you for nurturing and guidance." Serena smiles as she departs.

Serena

Dosage: In the morning, once a week

River Release

Clearing the path for increased clarity and Angelic wisdom begins by using this visualization. Imagine you are at the bank of a river, concentrating on the sound of water rushing over the large rocks. Now, using hand motions, release into the river all of the thoughts and feelings that are keeping you from believing in yourself. Take the time to let go of everything that is undesirable. See Archangel Uriel standing on the other side, smiling and nodding his approval while he witnesses this process. Proud of you for having cleared the way to receiving additional insight, he extends an invitation to come back as often as possible. When the scene fades away, know that you have been given Archangel Uriel's gift of awareness. He sends his spiritual blessings to fill your future with enlightenment.

Dosage: Daily for ten days, then as desired

Beach Sunset

This visualization enhances feelings of serenity and inner peace. Picture yourself on a beach with cool sand beneath your feet. The sun is beginning to set, as beautiful orange and yellow hues paint the sky. The Earth's horizon is filled with a warm glow. William, the Angel of Peace, approaches, inspiring awe with his presence. Notice how strong, yet friendly, he appears. The Angel smiles and says, "I will be your guide to inner peace by taking you along the path to tranquility." Incredible joy and serenity now fill your body upon hearing these words. William raises his hand in blessing as he leaves you in perfect harmony.

Dosage: As desired

Moonlit Night

To experience the love of God through meditation, visualize yourself standing in the middle of a moonlit night with the stars twinkling above. Joseph, the Angel of Joy, is in the background looking peaceful. A beam of divine light shines down from the sky, showering you with its radiance. God is bathing you in His love. Hold the feeling of bliss for at least one minute. Continue to bask in the moonlight before leaving this glorious scene. After the visualization, carry this loving experience in your heart forever.

Dosage: At night, three times a week

Angelic Adventure

If you are an advanced seeker of truth or would like to be one, use this visualization to develop a more personal relationship with the Angels. Imagine Archangel Michael available to be your escort to the Angelic Realm. While wrapped in his arms, you feel yourself being lifted to a higher level of consciousness. Upon arriving, see the Angels going about all their celestial activities. They extend warm, welcoming greetings. Allow the peace and serenity of your surroundings to fill you with joy. Stay for as long as you like and visit often. Angels are great hosts and love company. When ready to depart from this Angelic Adventure, Archangel Michael will be your guide on the return trip. Having a closer relationship with the Celestial Beings creates a happier future.

Dosage: As desired for spiritual enlightenment

Golden Temple

The purpose of this exercise is to enhance a sense of inner peace and the feeling of being supported in all your endeavors. Start by doing the *Breathing Technique (Career)*. Next, envision yourself ascending a beautiful staircase that leads to a golden temple. As you walk through the magnificent doors, glance in each direction. The room is comfortable, with white candles glowing throughout. Velvet cushions have been placed against the wall. Select one and seat yourself in the center of the room. Call on the Angels to join you. Acknowledge the tranquility that comes from having them at your side. Concentrate on bliss and ask to be blessed with clarity and wisdom. Request God's guidance in identifying and fulfilling your life's purpose. Then, contemplate inner peace as the warmth, love and faith within you begin to grow. Revel in this experience.

When ready to leave the temple, walk back to the staircase where Lorena, the Angel of Divine Grace, is waiting to accompany you. She smiles lovingly, saying, "Come and visit the golden temple as often as you like."

Dosage: Once a week, or as desired

Preventative Medicine

Two remedies, two times a week

Two affirmations, three times a week

Angel of the Sea©

CAREER

How Angel First Aid Helps You Advance Your Career

Individuals who can successfully meld a career path with their life's purpose achieve the ultimate satisfaction. Everyone has talents that lead to the fulfillment of personal and professional goals. When using these special gifts or on a course to developing them, there is a much greater potential for increasing prosperity.

Angel First Aid for Career enlists the assistance of the Angels in identifying and pursuing your ideal profession.

Angel Specialists

Archangel Gabriel

Bettina	Angel of Creativity
Cory	Angel of Career Development
James	Angel of Public Speaking
Loretta	Angel of New Enterprise
Nancy	Angel of Productivity
Perrie	Angel of Music
Phillip	Angel of Employment
Rebecca	Angel of Self-Confidence
Rita	Angel of Writing

Affirmations

I am supported by the Angels.

I am filled with optimism and hope.

I have a career that brings me joy.

I am using all my special talents.

I am competent and responsible.

I have a job that fulfills my goals.

I am being rewarded for my efforts.

I am making a good impression.

I have an enjoyable, prosperous career.

Case Study

Debbie, an executive in her forties, had been employed by a large utility company. Due to downsizing, her position was eliminated. She then began a year-long search for a job that would support her life's purpose – one that utilized the creative and artistic talents she had worked hard to develop.

It was difficult staying optimistic when letters of rejection arrived, so I used Angel First Aid exercises to maintain a positive outlook. Career Bliss helped me to focus on what kind of job would be best while Interview Preview kept my spirits up. I constantly visualized being a "winner" and everyone was amazed by my upbeat attitude. Working with the techniques from Angel First Aid for Business and Money during the day and repeating affirmations at night before going to sleep was an important part of my routine.

Out of the blue, a headhunter called and offered me a well-paying executive position that used all my creative talents. I just wanted to pinch myself to make sure that it was true. Everything is perfect!

Remedies

Angel Scrapbook

Individuals are born with unique qualities and talents that indicate their life's purpose. These special gifts usually become apparent at a young age. Ask the Angels to help you put together a scrapbook of early experiences that reveals your natural abilities.

Recalling past memories will help to determine what was special about you before the age of five. Looking at a family photo album may be helpful. Question parents and relatives for clues that will pinpoint your inherent attributes. Begin picturing the events where these special gifts were first used.

Now, place them in an imaginary scrapbook and ask Cory, the Angel of Career Development, to reveal professions that would best utilize your unique abilities. This remedy is important in finding job success, so keep the scrapbook handy and share it frequently with the Angels.

Dosage: Once a day

Yes or No

To determine a career that would be the most enjoyable, use this exercise. With the Angels looking on, place the fingertips of each hand on your breastbone. After choosing a career, make a simple statement to help you discover if this is the correct one. Here's an example: think about becoming a computer programmer and say,

"A job as a computer programmer is the right one for me." If you begin to move forward, the answer is yes. A backward movement is an indication that there is a better position available.

The body's intelligence also provides answers to similar questions in other areas of your life. When you are making a decision, the Angels encourage using this remedy as a guidance tool.

Dosage: Daily, until you have the perfect job

Career Bliss

To manifest professional goals, declare your intentions to the Angels. Invite Cory, the Angel of Career Development, to be your guide for this adventure.

Think about what it would be like to land the perfect job. Imagine standing in the basket of a hot air balloon that sets down at the location of the new position. As you begin looking around, observe every detail related to this job – responsibilities, personalities of your colleagues, how management operates, the working environment and anything else of importance. Actually see your office, its location, furnishings and number of windows. Let Cory escort you on a tour of the new surroundings. He shares your enthusiasm and excitement. When you are ready to leave, allow Cory to navigate the return trip. His parting words are, "Watch for Angelic help in making your dream job a reality."

Dosage: As needed, until employed

Interview Preview

Allow the Angels to help in building your self-esteem. They want you to be a "winner." Having this attitude is an asset in achieving career goals. Perform the following technique just before going on an interview.

Imagine walking down a theater aisle toward the stage. Climb the stairs onto the platform where seven Angels are waiting to place a wide ribbon with a gold medal around your neck. Turn to face the audience. Everyone is standing and applauding. You are feeling victorious and proud to be recognized for your accomplishments. Hold the exhilaration of this moment for one minute. Then, leave the stage and walk down the aisle past the audience. Keep smiling as each person shakes your hand and offers congratulations.

Dosage: Three times a day, or before an interview

Search Booster

Once you have decided on your ideal career path and have done the basics required for a successful job search – such as updating a resume, talking to recruiters and actively seeking interviews – give your efforts an Angelic boost.

To receive guidance and direction from the Celestial Beings, use the following affirmations: *"I am living my life's purpose,"* and *"I have a harmonious relationship with success."* Let Phillip, the Angel of Employment, know you would be honored to accept his advice and support in your quest for a new job. Then, watch and listen for the divine suggestions that will be coming your way.

Dosage: Daily

Breathing Technique

This breathing technique is especially helpful before an interview or for relieving job-related stress. Invite the Angels to be nearby. Breathe in through your nose and follow the air as it travels down the spine to your tailbone. Leave some of the air in your tailbone, then exhale through your mouth. Repeat the exercise three times.

Dosage: Whenever needed to stay calm

Angel Notes: This technique can be performed before beginning a visualization or doing a remedy. Use it to relax in a stressful situation or to regain poise and control.

Confidence Builder

The Angels realize that being confident and alert creates the best possible impression while on an interview. Try this technique for an energy boost.

Take your dominant hand and rub it across the lower part of your rib cage seven times (a movement back and forth counts as one). Then, cross your arms over your chest, grasping the upper arms just under the shoulders. Use your fingertips to briskly rub up and down seven times. Next, place your hands on the outside of your thighs. Apply slight pressure. Then, move them from hip to knee seven times. Notice how energized and empowered you feel. By doing this exercise, you will stand out from the other candidates, appearing more capable and confident.

Dosage: As desired for extra energy

Angel Notes: Use this technique to increase body strength and improve your health. You may notice tingling or better posture as a result.

Positive Focus

If the job search is not progressing as quickly as you wish, enlist the help of the Angels. Since their blessings are aligned with your best interests, they will find the most ideal opportunities for you. Keep a positive attitude. Write a career vision statement, reading it often. Begin by focusing on your goals and practicing various *Angel First Aid* exercises. The remedies listed in the chapters on Happiness and Money would be best. Then, joyfully continue the search. Stay upbeat and trust in the Angels' guidance.

Dosage: As needed

Preventative Medicine:

Two remedies, three times a week
One affirmation, three times a week

BUSINESS

How Angel First Aid Helps You in Business

S uccessful business owners have a vision which they support by their actions. With assistance from the Angels, executives can gain clarity for setting goals and implementing effective plans. Celestial Beings will serve as around-the-clock partners for networking and increasing a company's client base. The Angels can contribute to entrepreneurial endeavors, creating greater success for small or home-based enterprises.

Angel First Aid for Business will assist in motivating you to build a strong foundation for excellence.

Angel Specialists

Archangel Gabriel

Alexander	Angel of Invention
Caroline	Angel of Positive Thinking
Cornell	Angel of Decision-Making
Loretta	Angel of New Enterprise
Nancy	Angel of Productivity
Randolph	Angel of Expansion
Raymond	Angel of Technology
Trevor	Angel of Stocks

Affirmations

I am creating abundance in my life.

I have great leadership abilities.

I am wealthy and financially secure.

I am accomplishing all my goals.

I have permission to be successful.

I have a growing, prosperous business.

I am learning something new each day.

I am compatible with my colleagues.

I have a happy work environment.

I have the self-confidence to succeed.

Case Study

Roger's company was experiencing financial difficulty. He had to make serious decisions that would ultimately affect his career and the rest of his life.

Three options were all that seemed feasible to me. I could sell my business outright, retain ownership of the company and cut costs, or find new ways to generate immediate cash. Asking the Angels for help and knowing they were guiding me was very important. The first thing I did was look for what was blocking my progress and stressing me out. While using Angel First Aid Techniques, I practiced Blackboard, then moved on to Picture of Success and Law of Increase. After having consulted with Randolph, the Angel of Expansion, everything changed for the better. Sales rose, and within nine months, my company was in the black. I even took a risk and made an offer on another business. Having less tension and more motivation encouraged me to share my success with others. With the Angels on my team, it's a win-win situation!

Remedies

Vision Statement

It is important that entrepreneurs have a vision statement. Utilize the Angels as advisors to determine what would contribute most to the growth of the company. Outline your intentions listing the results you desire. An example of an effective vision statement is: *"I am using my special talents to create a successful business. My expertise is an asset to clients. I am being handsomely rewarded for my efforts."* After the statement has been perfected, be sure to write it down. Since Angels enjoy being involved in the creative process, call on them to start making your goals a reality.

Dosage: Repeat three times a day

Blackboard

Angels know success can be sabotaged when people hold on to limiting beliefs. This exercise is offered as a means to free yourself from counterproductive thoughts making way for progressive ideas. Imagine standing in front of a blackboard. Take a piece of chalk and write the messages you want removed, such as fear of failure, lack of financial

support and feelings of unworthiness. Eliminate these thoughts by washing off the board with an imaginary power hose. Do not use an eraser as it may leave specks. When the board is clean, breathe a sigh of relief. Now, using a piece of colorful chalk, write goals you envision for yourself. These statements reflect the opposite messages of those removed from the board, for example, *"I have success," "I am financially secure,"* and *"I have self-confidence."* Affirmations such as *"I am building a thriving business"* can be included. Leave all these positive statements on the board. For the best results, repeat them often while accepting Angelic guidance for success and prosperity.

Dosage: Once a day

Angel Notes: This exercise may be modified for use in other areas of your life to remove limiting beliefs and create beneficial results.

Goal Setting

Each morning, list your goals on a sheet of paper. Across the top, write, *"Angel miracles fill my day."* Include all the details such as how much you want to earn and the number of clients that would be advantageous. Add the necessary particulars that could make your day successful. Be realistic, yet focus on growth. Keep the paper where you can refer to it easily and repeat the goals often. Trust that your partners from the Angelic Realm are busy helping to create miraculous results.

Dosage: Daily, in the morning

Color Me Successful

To strengthen personal power and the stability of your company, imagine Nancy, the Angel of Productivity, standing nearby. She has a pitcher filled with the colors of a rainbow. The Angel begins to pour them slowly, one-by-one, over the crown of your head. As they flow down through your body, notice that you are becoming stronger. Nancy then adds a radiant white light to fortify the colors working to empower you. While envisioning the company's success, hold this thought for at least one minute. As the Angel leaves, you become motivated and much more energetic.

Dosage: Four times a week

Law of Increase

To "grow your business" and improve its profitability, employ the **Law of Increase**. Invite the Angels to be present as you make this pledge. Enthusiastically say, *"I invoke the Law of Increase!"* The Celestial Beings will bring this promise to fruition. Imagine your declaration being heard by all the Angels.

Dosage: Three times a day

Expand Your Territory

For manifesting a successful and productive enterprise, Randolph, the Angel of Expansion, will contribute his expertise to increasing your company's territory. First, picture a map that encompasses an ideal area for your business. Then, highlight in a medium blue the current geographical boundaries. Visualize all the lines expanding to meet the larger dimensions that coincide with your company's vision for the future. The Angels now know where their blessings are needed and how they can be most effective. This technique is very powerful when used consistently.

Dosage: Daily

Picture of Success

Enlist the involvement of Angels in raising the bottom line. Begin by visualizing a painting representing your five-year plan. Include the vision statement. Think of sounds such as telephones ringing and employees making appointments or taking orders. Frame the picture in orange and imagine how elated you will feel as profits begin to rise. Focus on this uplifting scene for one minute. Revel in the excitement that develops as you envision being financially rewarded for your efforts. Now, enlarge the painting until it fills the room. The Angels see the work of art and start the process of creating success.

Dosage: Daily

Preventative Medicine:

Two remedies, two times a week
Three affirmations, three times a week

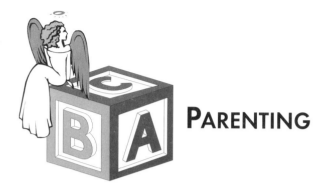

PARENTING

How Angel First Aid Helps You Become a Better Parent

C hildren who communicate with the Angels grow into the healthiest, happiest and most productive adults. Parents can give their youngsters a priceless gift by encouraging them to develop relationships with these loving and supportive beings. Angels will help children build their self-confidence as well as motivate them to excel.

Angel First Aid for Parenting offers you guidance on nurturing your child's connection with the Angels.

Angel Specialists

Archangel Uriel

Eileen	Angel of Happiness
Jacob	Angel of Education
Kevin	Angel of Friendship
Melody	Angel of Self-Esteem
Nancy	Angel of Productivity
Patrick	Angel of Sports
Rebecca	Angel of Self-Confidence
Serena	Angel of Children
Tara	Angel of Love

Affirmations

I am a good parent.

I am understanding.

I have healthy children.

I am listening to my child.

I am proud of my child.

I have happy, loving children.

I am happy that my child is doing well.

I am able to give and receive love.

I have children who are blessed by Angels.

Case Study

Sarah and Larry had been trying to have a baby for many years. Longing for a child of her own, Sarah was very happy when she and her husband finally made the decision to adopt.

The day that we went to get our beautiful daughter, Lynne, from the adoption agency, the social worker said, "Use loving words every morning to help your child feel secure and accepted." We wanted to do everything to make Lynne's life happy, so Larry and I followed this important advice.

As our daughter was growing up, I began using the Melody's Gift visualization to boost her self-confidence. During Lynne's early years, I called on Jacob, the Angel of Education, to help with her studies and provide support. Lynne was an exceptional student, winning a special presidential award for academic achievement. Graduating from college with honors, she is now following her dream sharing "loving words" through writing children's books.

Remedies

Plenty

The Angels encourage children to believe that unlimited resources are available. To reinforce this idea, instruct them to say the word "plenty" often. Make it into a game, poem, or song. The following is a simple rhyme they can recite.

There is ...

> *Plenty of time for you and me,*
> *Plenty of places for us to see,*
> *Plenty of love that we can share,*
> *Plenty of happiness everywhere.*

The Plenty remedy is a favorite of Serena and the other Angels. Have your children say or sing "Plenty" before they go to bed. This is also a good activity to use during car trips or vacations.

Dosage: Every day for a month, or as desired

Angel Notes: Bring abundance into your life by singing or saying this rhyme with your children. Compose a personal poem and use the word "plenty" all the time.

Inside Out

The Angels know that being a parent can be quite challenging and trying. This simple technique will help you keep your composure. Visualize the difficult child standing in front of you, accompanied and protected by a Guardian Angel. Focus on the reason for being upset. Then, take a deep breath and blow quickly and vigorously in the child's direction. Repeat five times. When you blow the air out, notice the anger and frustration leaving your body. Continue with the remedy until relief is experienced and patience begins to return. Utilizing Inside Out as a means to "clear the air" creates a physiological reaction that reduces stress. Teaching this technique to children will enable them to identify and release unhealthy and unproductive emotions.

Dosage: Whenever necessary

Angel Notes: Inside Out is an easy, effective way to modify your behavior in an effort to have more positive interactions with other people. It can be practiced in most places. However, if you are in a situation where it is not practical or appropriate, then visualize performing the remedy.

Hand Hold

Using this technique provides children with a sense of safety and security. It also helps to keep them calm. Begin by folding your hand over the child's fingertips. Then, using mild pressure, push down toward the wrist seven times. Repeat this procedure on the thumb. Duplicate the process on the other hand. Next, place your open hand, palm down, on the crown of the child's head pressing firmly, yet gently, seven times. For a small child, this process can also be used on shoulders, knees, elbows and toes. Applied often, this exercise is extremely effective for balancing mind and body.

Dosage: As needed

Angel Notes: Playing Baroque music while using Hand Hold is particularly effective for children with Attention Deficit Disorder, dyslexia, learning disabilities, allergies and asthma.

Angel Prayer

Teach your children to recite the following rhyme before saying their prayers at night. It will help them connect with the Angels.

> *God is great,*
> *God is good,*
> *God is everywhere.*
> *Please bend down,*
> *And kiss my crown,*
> *And listen to my prayer.*

Melody's Gift

To build their self-esteem, guide children through this visualization. Have them envision a lovely Angel named Melody. She has large, white wings and sparkling blue eyes. The color of her long, flowing dress is a beautiful yellow. Ask the youngsters to think about what makes them special and share these qualities and talents with Melody. The children are proud and happy that they are blessed with so many unique gifts. Have them use their imagination to see the pretty Angel bringing a "pretend gift" to unwrap and enjoy. Instruct the children to wave good-bye when Melody leaves. This is an excellent time to give the youngsters praise for their accomplishments.

Taking note of your children's best attributes provides valuable insight into the divine purposes of their lives.

Dosage: Three times per week

Angel Tutors

Suggest that your children ask their Angels for help with school work, sports and other interests. Encourage them to talk to Jacob, the Angel of Education, or Patrick, the Angel of Sports. Imagine these Celestial Beings blessing your youngsters with the ability to perform well and excel in everything they do. Feel confident that protection and guidance from the Angels will be provided.

Dosage: As desired, more during the school year

Letting Go

Learning to handle anger helps children to be more peaceful and content. Those who accept, understand and work effectively with this emotion grow up to become happier, more productive adults.

Tell the youngsters that they can throw away their angry thoughts and feelings. Have them start by imagining a trash can. Now, with Eileen, the Angel of Happiness, at their side, describe how to get rid of anger by tossing it into the empty can. Suggest that they use hand motions as if shooting a basket. When finished disposing of these thoughts and feelings, have the children visualize the trash being hauled away in a truck driven by Angels. Everyone waves good-bye. Use this remedy together with the children for several weeks. Then, encourage them to practice it on their own.

Dosage: As needed

Preventative Medicine

One remedy, two times a week
One affirmation, three times a week

SERENA'S TALE

Serena, the Guardian Angel of Children, would like to share this wonderful story about a technique and the impression it made on a young child.

Carolyn, a lively, precocious three-year-old, was naturally curious while watching her mother, Brenda, using the Letting Go remedy. When her daughter asked to try the exercise, Brenda was pleased. She modified the remedy and gave her these simple instructions: "Cup your hands and put anything that makes you angry in them." Carolyn did this with her undivided attention.

Several days later, when she saw Brenda growing angry, Carolyn cupped her hands, getting them ready to start receiving thoughts. "Mommy," the concerned little girl said, "Put your Mad in here."

Serena's Angel Notes: *The best thing you can do for children is let them watch you make positive changes in your own life. This gives children permission to do the same.*

PETS

How Angel First Aid Helps You Care for Your Pets

Pets play a very important role in people's lives. Much like Angels, they are loyal, devoted companions who provide unconditional love and affection. Animals bring great joy to people with their playfulness and boundless energy. Learning how to nurture pets shows appreciation for having them as a part of the family.

Angel First Aid for Pets offers guidance to enhancing comfort and well-being in animals.

Angel Specialists

Archangel Michael

Blake	Angel of Comfort
Eileen	Angel of Happiness
Joseph	Angel of Joy
Kevin	Angel of Friendship
Laramie	Angel of Discovery
Sarah	Angel of Harmony
Tara	Angel of Love
Theodore	Angel of Kindness
Thomas	Angel of Animal Care

Affirmations

My pet brings me joy and happiness.

I am understanding of my pet's needs.

My pet is always safe and secure.

I am playing and having fun with my pet.

My pet is healing and growing stronger.

I am loving and enjoying my pet.

My pet receives the love of the Angels.

Case Study

There are special pets that people just know are Angels. Twinkles is one of these animals – understanding and unique in many ways. Marianne has shared with me incredible stories about this cat and the close relationship they have.

One windy night the front door blew open and Twinkles ran out. Marianne was worried because the cat was declawed and unable to protect itself.

Twinkles is a black cat and it was midnight. Searching for her this late was futile. Needless to say, I was in a real panic. My first step was to ask Laramie, the Angel of Discovery, for help. Then, I got the idea to open all the doors to the house and try using the Lost Pet remedy. Visualizing Twinkles curled up on her favorite chair in the living room was a thought that never left my mind. Within twenty minutes, she scurried through the door and jumped on her chair. Overjoyed, I rushed to open a can of cat food which she ate quickly. After eating, she jumped onto my lap and soon was fast asleep. Using the Pet Well-Being remedy for soothing, I rubbed her neck until she purred. Laramie was my hero for guiding my precious pet back home.

Remedies

Pet Bonding

The Angels love pets. They enjoy the affection that people share with these animals. One rewarding way to bond with a pet is by using mind-to-mind communication. Looking deeply into  your pet's eyes, concentrate on the love you feel. Now, send your message through the eyes of the animal to its mind. Then, notice if there is a change. Are you receiving a signal of love in return? A purr or lick is a good sign.

To expand on this exercise, practice communicating with the pet while it is in another room. In your mind, call out its name seven times. Then, visualize your thoughts traveling as a beam of light to the animal's forehead. Does your pet come to you? Practice the skill daily to develop a more lasting bond between the two of you.

Dosage: As desired

Touch of Love

Use this remedy if your pet needs healing. Put your hands around the middle of its body until your fingertips touch. Next, imagine Angels pouring blessings into the crown of your head, allowing the energy to flow down through your neck, shoulders, arms and hands into the animal's body. It is common for a person's palms to start to feel warm. Now, see the pet being filled with medium blue. This color generates additional energy. Be sure to allow at least seven minutes for each healing session. When working with larger animals, place your hands directly on the area that needs attention. For fish, your palms go up against the outside of the aquarium. Birds are held or receive healing through their cage.

Dosage: Repeat as often as necessary

Pet Well-Being

Ask the Angels to be present. Then, begin using this technique to create love and warmth for your cat or dog. Place the three middle fingers of your dominant hand on the back of the pet's neck and rub vigorously, yet gently. Your fingertips never move more than two inches in any direction. This is an Angelic remedy that instills a sense of comfort in your pet.

Dosage: Two times a day

Pet Healing

To generate special healing power for a pet, start by imagining the animal in perfect health. Picture yourself with the pet playing and having a good time. Envision Thomas, the Angel of Animal Care, joining in the fun. He is sprinkling sparkling blue dust on the pet, especially concentrating on problem areas. Hold this picture for at least one minute, while trusting that improvement in the animal's health is on the way.

Dosage: As often as needed

Angel Notes: Like you, pets have Angels for love and protection. Call upon these Celestial Beings at any time for their blessings.

Lost Pet

Laramie, the Angel of Discovery, loves animals and is happy to be of assistance whenever a pet is missing. Ask the Angels to deliver the animal to you safe and sound. Then, imagine your pet being in its favorite place while feeling the joy of having the animal home with you again.

Dosage: Three times a day for a lost pet

Missed Pets

Do this remedy if you are grieving the passing of a cherished pet. Close your eyes and picture the animal being nurtured by Angels. Using the pet's name, verbally express love and gratitude for the joy it brought to your family. Then, relax and feel a great sense of peace and comfort, knowing that your close companion is being cared for by the Angels.

Dosage: As needed

Preventative Medicine:

Two remedies, three times a week
Three affirmations, two times a week

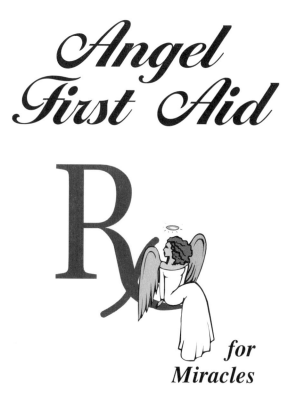

Angel First Aid

Rx for Miracles

This book is about love, happiness and prosperity. Its purpose is to awaken you to the realization that miracles are happening in people's lives all the time.

The key messages to remember after reading *Angel First Aid* are: *there is always hope* and *you are never alone*. So, watch for little miracles, as they announce the presence of Angels. When you notice them, express your gratitude and be open to receiving more. The Angels want to make all things possible for you. Invite them into your life.

GLOSSARY OF ANGELS

Archangels

Gabriel: Delivers messages. Works with arts, invention and communication.

Michael: Provides guidance and protection. Inspires divine justice.

Raphael: Accelerates healing and compassion. Promotes brotherhood.

Uriel: Inspires spirituality and enlightenment. Encourages prosperity.

Angel Specialists

Alan, Angel of Investments: Nurtures financial growth. Contributes to sound decision-making.

Alexander, Angel of Invention: Inspires ideas. Creates development of products.

Allison, Angel of Plants: Supports growth of healthy plants. Helps to develop a green thumb.

Barry, Angel of Strength: Provides endurance. Supplies emotional support.

Bettina, Angel of Creativity: Inspires divine gifts in arts, sciences and business.

Blake, Angel of Comfort: Orchestrates blessings for physical ease and peace of mind.

Cameron, Angel of Weather: Brings nice weather. Provides support and protection during storms.

Caroline, Angel of Positive Thinking: Affirms productive, healthy, successful thoughts.

Cornell, Angel of Decision-Making: Develops ability to evaluate information.

Cory, Angel of Career Development: Builds strong productive careers. Creates prosperity.

Darrin, Angel of Housing: Expedites buying and selling of homes. Finds comfortable living spaces.

Diane, Angel of Childcare: Provides competent, loving care for children.

Eileen, Angel of Happiness: Gathers sources of joy and contentment.

Evelyn, Angel of Manifesting: Attracts wealth, prosperity and personal growth.

Florence, Angel of Compassion: Brings kindness and understanding. Works with health.

Gunther, Angel of Fitness: Provides energy and discipline. Supports exercise programs.

Jacob, Angel of Education: Develops knowledge for advancement in learning and performance.

James, Angel of Public Speaking: Brings success to speakers. Bolsters confidence.

Jeremiah, Angel of Financial Security: Builds solid foundations for material growth.

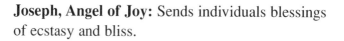

Joseph, Angel of Joy: Sends individuals blessings of ecstasy and bliss.

Katrina, Angel of Prosperity: Provides success with money, health and happiness.

Kevin, Angel of Friendship: Improves skills for communication. Creates cooperation.

Laramie, Angel of Discovery: Searches for lost people, objects and pets.

Lorena, Angel of Divine Grace: Delivers a great wealth of spiritual blessings and enrichment.

Loretta, Angel of New Enterprises: Oversees endeavors related to career and business.

Lucien, Angel of Resources: Creates opportunity for prosperity, wealth and joy.

Marilyn, Angel of Leisure: Provides sources for play, fun and relaxation.

Maureen, Angel of Time: Makes adequate time for work activities and travel.

Melody, Angel of Self-Esteem: Sparks internal recognition of value and potential.

Mirra, Angel of Healing Arts: Offers support through education. Promotes compassion.

Nancy, Angel of Productivity: Increases output and performance.

Pamela, Angel of Environment: Supports life for humans, nature and the planet.

Patrick, Angel of Sports Achievement: Helps participants with athletic activities and dancing.

Perrie, Angel of Music: Enhances musical talent. Bestows blessings on the arts.

Peter, Angel of Health: Improves energy and balance for physical well-being.

Phillip, Angel of Employment: Creates desirable work situations. Supports career changes.

Rachel, Angel of Inspiration: Delivers divine, creative and uplifting messages.

Raymond, Angel of Technology: Works with computers and electronic devices.

Rebecca, Angel of Self-Confidence: Bolsters and strengthens self-esteem.

Rex, Angel of Cars: Works with mechanics. Oversees automobile performance.

Rita, Angel of Writing: Clears thoughts. Provides focus for written material.

Robert, Angel of Balance: Helps achieve stability, equilibrium and peace of mind.

Robin, Angel of Social Contact: Organizes social events and outings. Arranges meetings of friends and dates.

Ruth, Angel of Divine Justice: Settles disputes. Guides toward equitable resolutions.

Sarah, Angel of Harmony: Promotes caring peaceful and blessed interactions.

Serena, Angel of Children: Nurtures, loves and protects children.

Solomon, Angel of Security: Bolsters sense of safety and well-being.

Susan, Angel of Travel: Sparks yearning to explore. Provides protection when traveling.

Tara, Angel of Love: Carries divine blessings of unconditional love and nurturing.

Terina, Angel of Attraction: Finds soul mates. Brings support and romance.

Theodore, Angel of Kindness: Develops warmth and affection in relationships.

Thomas, Angel of Animal Care: Provides safety, protection and comfort to animals.

Timothy, Angel of Good Fortune: Bestows many blessings of abundance and prosperity.

Trevor, Angel of Stocks: Guides in evaluating market information. Provides success.

William, Angel of Peace: Emits blessings of love, joy and harmony.

REMEDIES BY CHAPTER

Prosperity

Angel Love
Time Prosperity
The Judge
Backbone
Golden Cylinder
Prosperity Painting
Colors of Balance
Merry-Go-Round

Relationships

Expanding Heart
Statement for Love
Likes Attract
Blue Sphere
Enhancing Relationships
Forgiveness

Money

True Money Beliefs
Money Memory
Plug Money Leaks
Stacking Cash
Plenty Exercise
Play Money
Money, Money Everywhere
Money Smiles
Dollar Sign
Wealth Affirmation

Remedies by Chapter (continued)

Health

Energy Tap

Vitality Plus

Healthy Body

Power of Eight

Medium Blue

Wastebasket

Picture of Health

Happiness

Forest Stream

Body Laugh

Twisting

Voice Mail

Sack of Gold

Smiley Balloon

Inner Peace

Serena's Embrace

River Release

Beach Sunset

Moonlit Night

Angelic Adventure

Golden Temple

<u>*Remedies by Chapter (continued)*</u>

Career

Angel Scrapbook
Yes or No
Career Bliss
Interview Preview
Search Booster
Breathing Technique
Confidence Builder
Positive Focus

Business

Vision Statement
Blackboard
Goal Setting
Color Me Successful
Law of Increase
Expand Your Territory
Picture of Success

Remedies by Chapter (continued)

Parenting

Plenty

Inside Out

Hand Hold

Angel Prayer

Melody's Gift

Angel Tutors

Letting Go

Prosperity
Relationships
Money
Health
Happiness
Inner Peace
Career
Business
Parenting
Pets

Pets

Pet Bonding

Touch of Light

Pet Well-being

Pet Healing

Lost Pet

Missed Pets

INDEX

This index is a partial list of remedies you can use according to the referenced *keyword*. Consider the optimal outcome you would like to achieve. Look up the *keyword* that describes the symptom or desired solution. Then, locate the suggested remedies that are referenced. Identify the remedy name that would be of most help. Note the chapter title and page number where it appears.

*Best one to use

Chapter Order: Prosperity – Relationships – Money – Health – Happiness –
– Inner Peace – Career – Business – Parenting – Pets –

*Best one to use

Chapter Order: Prosperity – Relationships – Money – Health – Happiness –
– Inner Peace – Career – Business – Parenting – Pets –

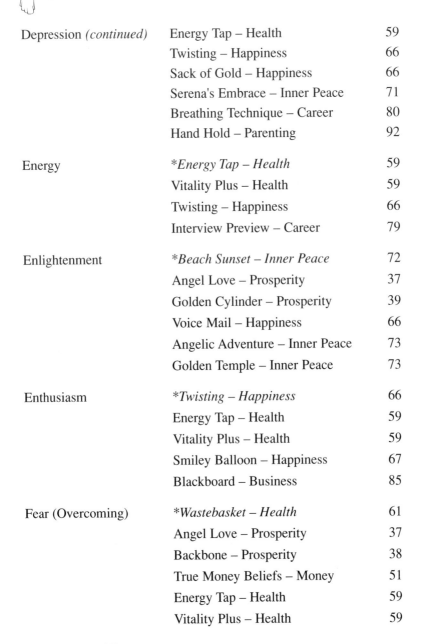

*Best one to use

Chapter Order: Prosperity – Relationships – Money – Health – Happiness –
– Inner Peace – Career – Business – Parenting – Pets –

Health & Well-being	*Breathing Technique – Career*	80
	Healthy Body – Health	59
	Medium Blue – Health	60
	Picture of Health – Health	61
	Pet Well-being – Pets	100
Inner Child (Healing)	*Wastebasket – Health*	61
	Expanding Heart – Relationships	45
	Statement for Love – Relationships	45
	Forgiveness – Relationships	48
	Money Memory – Money	51
	Sack of Gold – Happiness	66
	Serena's Embrace – Inner Peace	71
	Breathing Technique – Career	80
	Plenty – Parenting	91
	Hand Hold – Parenting	92
Inner Peace	*Sack of Gold – Happiness*	66
	Angel Love – Prosperity	37
	Colors of Balance – Prosperity	40
	Smiley Balloon – Happiness	67
	Entire Chapter – Inner Peace	71
Joy	*Sack of Gold – Happiness*	66
	Wastebasket – Health	61
	Entire Chapter – Happiness	65
Learning Disabilities	*Hand Hold – Parenting*	92
	Entire Chapter – Health	59
	Twisting – Happiness	66
	Breathing Technique – Career	80

*Best one to use

Chapter Order: Prosperity – Relationships – Money – Health – Happiness – – Inner Peace – Career – Business– Parenting – Pets –

*Best one to use

Chapter Order: Prosperity – Relationships – Money – Health – Happiness – – Inner Peace – Career – Business – Parenting – Pets –

Soul Mate	*Blue Sphere - Relationships*	46
	Angel Love – Prosperity	37
	Golden Cylinder – Prosperity	39
	Likes Attract – Relationships	46
	Interview Preview – Career	79
Strength	*Merry-Go-Round – Prosperity*	40
	Backbone – Prosperity	38
	Colors of Balance – Prosperity	40
	Interview Preview – Career	79
	Color Me Successful – Business	86
Stress (Overcoming)	*Angel Love – Prosperity*	37
	Serena's Embrace – Inner Peace	71
	Breathing Technique – Career	80
	Inside Out – Parenting	91
	Hand Hold – Parenting	92
Success	*Goal Setting – Business*	86
	Backbone – Prosperity	38
	Prosperity Painting – Prosperity	39
	Interview Preview – Career	79
	Search Booster – Career	79
	Color Me Successful – Business	86
	Picture of Success – Business	88
Support	*Voice Mail – Happiness*	66
	Angel Love – Prosperity	37
	Backbone – Prosperity	38
	Smiley Balloon – Happiness	67

Best one to use

Chapter Order: Prosperity – Relationships – Money – Health – Happiness –
– Inner Peace – Career – Business – Parenting – Pets –

CONTACTING THE ANGEL LADY

The Angel Lady welcomes calls for Angelic Guidance.

Angelight Productions

1038 Whirlaway Avenue
Naperville, IL 60540
800-323-1790
630-420-1334
630-420-1474 (fax)
suestorm@earthlink.net
www.theangellady.net

When sending e-mail, please include a phone number.

Renaissance Angel ©

Angel Art by Joanne Koenig-Macko
630-579-8184 • joannem232@aol.com

Cover layout by DebManning Design
630-668-0603 • www.debmanning. com

Photograph by Stuart Pearson
815-726-5128 • stuartf8@aol.com